IMAGES
of America

KAUFMANN'S
DEPARTMENT STORE

D1073257

KAUFMANN'S
STORE DIRECTORY

A	FLOOR
Accessories	1
Alteration Pick Up	
Men's	2
Ladies	4
Auditorium	11

B	FLOOR
Baby Registry	5
Bake Shop	Arcade
Bath Shop	6
Beauty Salon	
Adoria	12
Elizabeth Arden	11
Quick Clip	4
Bedding	6
Better Sportswear	4
Books	9
Boy's Clothing	5
Bridal Registry	7

C	FLOOR
Candy	9
Cards and Wrap	
Hallmark	Arcade
Holiday	7
Carpet and Rugs	8
Children's	5
China	7
Christmas Shop	7
Coats	
Children's	5
Men's	2
Misses	5
Petites	4
Women's World	5
Cookware	7
Cosmetics	1
Crystal Gallery	7
Customer Service	
Credit	9
Cutlery	7

D	FLOOR
Dental Center	2
Domestics	6
Dresses	
Girl's	5
Juniors	5
Misses	4
Petites	4
Women's World	5
Dinnerware	7

E	FLOOR
Electronics	8
Employment Offices	12
Engraving, Jewelry	9

F	FLOOR
Fine Jewelry	1
Fragrances	1
Furniture	10
Fur Storage and	
Cleaning	6

G	FLOOR
Gift Certificates	2,9
Gifts and Collectibles	7
Gift Wrapping	1,3
Girl's Clothing	5
Glassware	7
Gloves	
Children's	5
Men's	1
Misses	1
Godiva	1,9
Gourmet Foods	9
Greeting Cards	Arcade

H	FLOOR
Handbags	1
Hilfiger	
Bedding and Towels	6
Boy's	5
Juniors	5
Men's	2
Misses	4
Hosiery	
Children's and	
Infants	5
Men's	1
Misses	1
Housewares	7

I	FLOOR
Infants and Toddler's	5
Intimate Apparel	6

J	FLOOR
Jewelry Departments	1
Jewelry Repair	9
Juniors	5

L	FLOOR
Ladies Sportswear	
Better Sportswear	4
Misses Blouses	
and Sweaters	3
Misses Coordinates	
and Separates	3
Misses Weekend	3
Petite Sportswear	4
Women's World	5
Linens	6
Lingerie	6
Lost and Found and	
Post Office	2
Luggage	8
Liz Claiborne	
Better Sportswear	4
Dresses	4
Men's Sportswear	2
Petite Sportswear	4
Women's World	5

M	FLOOR
Men's Clothing	
Coats & Outerwear	2
Suits & Sportcoats	2
Men's Fragrance's	1
Men's Furnishings	
Dress Shirts & Ties	1
Gifts and Jewelry	1
Hosiery	1
Underwear	1
Men's Sportswear	
Collections	2
Pants and Levi's	2
Sweaters and Shirts	2
Team Shop and	
Active	St Lvl
Misses Sportswear	3
Mattresses	10

O	FLOOR
OASIS Center	10
Optical Department	9

P	FLOOR
Petite Sportswear	4
Petite Dresses & Suits	4
Photo Studio	9
Picture Framing	9
Picture Frames	Arcade
Pillows	6
Post Office	2
Polo, Ralph Lauren	
Bedding and Towels	6
Boy's	5
China	7
Men's	2
Misses	4
Petites	4

R	FLOOR
Restaurants	
Block & Barrel	Skywalk
Café Nové	9
Deli	9
Edgar's	11
Forbes Room	11
Michael's	11
Temptations	9
Tic Toc	1
Rest Rooms	
Men's	2,9,11
Women's	3,5,9,11
Rugs	8

S	FLOOR
Santaland	7
Shoes	
Children's	5
Juniors	3
Men's	Arcade
Women's	3
Silverware	7
Skywalk	3
Small Electrics	7
Stationery	Arcade
Stereo and Electronics	8
Store Manager's Office	7

T	FLOOR
Telephones	8
Televisions	8
Tickets	9
Towels	6
Travel Service	9

U, V, W, Y	FLOOR
Umbrellas	1
Vacuum Cleaners	8
Watches	1
Watch Repair	9
Women's World	5
Young Men's	2

QUICK REFERENCE CHART

FLOOR	AREA	FLOOR	AREA
1	Accessories, Cosmetics, Men's Furnishings	6	Domestics, Intimate Apparel
Arcade	Bakery, Cards, Frames, Men's Shoes	7	Housewares, TableTop
2	Men's Sportswear, Men's Suits	8	Electronics, Rugs
3	Misses Sportswear, Shoes	9	Books, Candy, Customer Service, Optical, Photo Studio, Picture Framing, Travel, Watch Repair
4	Better and Petite Sportswear and Dresses	10	Furniture, OASIS
5	Children's, Coats, Juniors, Women's World	11	Auditorium, Beauty Salon, Restaurants

The location of departments in Kaufmann's downtown Pittsburgh flagship store changed frequently. The company published updated directories several times per year. This directory dates from late 1998. (Author's collection.)

ON THE COVER: Kaufmann's Department Store was a major shopping destination, especially for those who worked downtown. Here, pedestrians cross the intersection of Smithfield Street and Fifth Avenue in front of the Kaufmann's flagship store in the early 1970s. (Courtesy of the Senator John Heinz History Center's Detre Library & Archives.)

IMAGES
of America

KAUFMANN'S
DEPARTMENT STORE

Melanie Linn Gutowski
with the Sen. John Heinz History Center
Foreword by Rick Sebak

ARCADIA
PUBLISHING

Published by Arcadia Publishing
Charleston, South Carolina

Printed in the United States of America

Library of Congress Control Number: 2017936678

For all general information, please contact Arcadia Publishing:
Telephone 843-853-2070
Fax 843-853-0044
E-mail sales@arcadiapublishing.com
For customer service and orders:
Toll-Free 1-888-313-2665

Visit us on the Internet at www.arcadiapublishing.com

For Hugo and Victoria, who will only know
Kaufmann's through stories and pictures.

CONTENTS

FOREWORD

When I grew up in the suburban South Hills of Pittsburgh in the 1950s and early 1960s, there was no South Hills Village Mall. Back then, if you needed new clothes or furniture or presents or interesting food, you went shopping downtown. We could take the Shannon-Library streetcar, get off on Grant Street and just walk down Fifth Avenue. Kaufmann's was right there, the center of our urban universe.

Or my mom would drive us into town in our big orange Pontiac that she always parked in the Kaufmann's parking garage. We would enter the store at the mezzanine entrance at the corner of Cherry Way and Forbes Avenue. There was a bakery counter there for a while on that odd level between the grand first floor and the men's department on the second.

As a kid, meeting my great-aunts Mary or Anne (who both worked in the city) at the Tic Toc Restaurant on the first floor was the very height of elegance. Fruit salad with a scoop of sherbet in the middle.

I remember specific purchases like a double-breasted herringbone sport coat that my father suggested when I was in high school. It was very stylish, very "Carnaby Street" at the time. Later, I remember checking out expensive duds in the Yves Saint Laurent department that had its own entrance on Fifth Avenue.

I think I'm not alone. Many people who grew up in Western Pennsylvania remember the store, its elegant touches, its restaurants, the escalators that got older and more interesting as you went up and up. And every December, it was a sidewalk destination, a must-stop spot along Smithfield Street and up Fifth to see the animated Christmas windows.

There was a lot to love at Kaufmann's. And when I started to learn more about Pittsburgh history, I found the store and the Kaufmann family had interactions with many major figures, from Albert Einstein who stayed at their home on his first visit to Pittsburgh, to Frank Lloyd Wright who designed and built Fallingwater for them, to Pres. William Howard Taft, our portliest president, who was delighted that he could buy big men's clothing off the rack at the store.

Of course, there was some serious sadness when Kaufmann's changed its name to Macy's in 2006 and even more weeping and gnashing of teeth when the store closed in 2015, but I realized then that I hadn't done any serious shopping there in years. Nonetheless, I loved that store and its impact on this city.

So, we are all lucky that Melanie Linn Gutowski has written this history of the place, sharing photographs and stories, revealing unexpected items, reminding us what a grand place it really was, and giving us a place to revive and restore some memories. New businesses may move in to the building, and we may still meet under the Kaufmann's clock, but the shopping universe has changed, and we rely on volumes like this to reconnect us with all the floors of this beloved big department store.

—Rick Sebak

ACKNOWLEDGMENTS

My husband and I were married in the summer of 2006, at the very moment that Kaufmann's was undergoing a rebranding as Macy's, and so I became the last bride in my family to register at the store. That experience capped off many years of shopping at its various locations, for prom gowns and perfume and special gifts. I remember picking out the first "major" present for my then-boyfriend there, an electric razor. Somehow, putting that razor on my Kaufmann's charge meant we were serious. (By the time this book is published, we'll have been married 11 years.) In 2004, while working downtown, I spent hours and hours in the flagship store with a French friend, Caroline Mignon, who was living in Pittsburgh as an au pair. The first time I took her into the store, she marveled at the French makeup brands' willingness to feature deals and free gifts for American shoppers, something they weren't yet doing in the French market. Since she left town in early 2005, she never knew the building as anything other than "Kaufmann's," which in my opinion makes her a true Pittsburgher at heart. My mom would remind me to be sure to check the paper for coupons if I planned to go shopping after work; they were nearly always there.

This book is a valentine to Kaufmann's. While it's impossible to be truly comprehensive in any written volume on the 135 years of the store's history, I have endeavored to capture the essence of what made Kaufmann's special and what has endured in the minds of generations of Pittsburgh's residents, especially from the perspective of its shoppers.

I must first and foremost thank one of my readers, Marilyn Young, for putting the idea of this book into my brain. She wrote me following the publication of my first book, *Pittsburgh's Mansions*, to ask why no one had yet written a history of the store, which at that time was set to close in a matter of weeks. Once she brought it up, I wondered the same, and with her blessing, I embarked on this project.

The nitty gritty of this book wouldn't have happened without the excellent and cheerful help of librarian Mary Jones of the Detre Library & Archives at the Senator John Heinz History Center, as well as her colleagues archivist Carly Lough, library director John Paul Deley, and the many volunteers who put time into scanning many of the fantastic images you hold in your hand.

I would also like to thank my "image underwriters," some of the generous folks who contributed to my crowdfunding campaign for this book: Dina Linn, Rachel Sedmak, Katie Smith, Elizabeth Williams, Nancy Winget, and Chris Yakicic. Your support means so much.

I also owe thanks to Lisa Auel of the Pittsburgh Ballet Theatre, artist Linda Barnicott, Miriam Meislik of the University of Pittsburgh Archives Service Center, Clinton Piper of the Western Pennsylvania Conservancy, and the fabulous Rick Sebak for supporting my work and contributing the foreword for this book.

Finally—and certainly most importantly—I need to thank the family members who have supported all of my work unfailingly, particularly my husband, Marc, and my parents, Jack and Amy Linn, who contributed many hours of childcare over the course of this project. Thank you from the bottom of my heart.

Unless otherwise noted, all images in this book are published courtesy of the Senator John Heinz History Center's Detre Library & Archives.

INTRODUCTION

When a massive and artistically significant renovation of Kaufmann's Department Store's first floor was completed in 1930, the *Pittsburgh Sun-Telegraph* devoted a special supplement to it. The publication celebrated every aspect of the store's new look, from architectural elements to ornate fixtures and metalwork. The introduction of the supplement, titled "After Me Cometh the Builder," was based on Rudyard Kipling's 1903 poem "The Palace," in which a mason building a castle digs a foundation only to find the ruins of a previous one. The poem acknowledges the transience of time and the built environment and laments that one day the builder's own work will be repurposed as the basis of some future person's.

The story is at once sad and hopeful—sad that the past has been ruined and forgotten, and hopeful that one day the work of the present will become part of the future. The reporters of the *Sun-Telegraph* had no idea how prophetic their use of Kipling's words would become. Kaufmann's as a store and a brand no longer exists. Instead, it has been used as the ruins sustaining a new development of its former home, currently under construction as of this writing.

To many Pittsburghers, Kaufmann's is frozen in memories, be they childhood holidays spent waiting to visit Santa in Toyland, or downtown lunch breaks spent window shopping, or the giddy happiness of a bride choosing her new home's furnishings. The store seems preserved in those moments. But the truth is that the store and the company were always changing and evolving; making improvements for comfort or convenience, or to fulfill some latent ambition. What made it seem like it was the same place was its enduring symbol that outlasted generations: the building that still stands at Fifth Avenue and Smithfield Street and its magnificent clock. But even there, these memories are built on the ruins of a previous generation's: the current structure is actually the sixth Kaufmann's building to exist in what is now the city of Pittsburgh. But at least for that sixth store, with its name indelibly embossed into the terra-cotta tile on the façade, the memory of Kaufmann's can never truly fade away as long as the building stands. This book seeks to ensure that one day, when there is no living memory of the place, a new generation may know how fondly it was regarded in the minds of so many.

At its peak, Kaufmann's had over 50 stores in four states, the last of which was opened in 2005 in Homestead, Pennsylvania, at the Waterfront shopping complex. But the Kaufmann's empire began as small as one can imagine, with two itinerant peddlers in 19th-century Germany who decided to bring their trade and tailoring skills to America. Jacob and Isaac Kaufmann, sons of Abraham and Sarah Wolf Kaufmann, were the first of four brothers to emigrate from Germany in the mid-1800s. While their father was a successful cattle farmer and not a tailor, he instilled good business sense in his sons from a young age, particularly the concept of selling for low margins at high volume. The brothers' choice of profession was clearly preordained by some ancient family history: the word *kaufmann* means "merchant" in German.

Jacob, the first to emigrate in 1868, sold notions door-to-door and was joined a year later by younger brother Isaac. Together, the two came to cover a large area of Western Pennsylvania surrounding Pittsburgh and stretching all the way to Oil City. The pace of business soon outgrew their nomadic model, and by 1871, the brothers had established J. Kaufmann and Brother in the city of Birmingham, now Pittsburgh's South Side.

The late 19th century was truly the golden age of the department store, and Kaufmann's had many competitors in the Pittsburgh area. These included Boggs & Buhl in Allegheny City (now Pittsburgh's North Side); Mansmann's in East Liberty; and in downtown alone, Rosenbaum's, Frank & Seder, Gimbels, Kaufmann & Baer (run by the founders' own cousins), and of course, Joseph Horne Co. Later downtown competition included Saks Fifth Avenue, Lord & Taylor, and Lazarus. In setting itself apart, Kaufmann's was proud to welcome all through its doors with its claim of "wholesale to the public." This tactic, along with the timely sale of the company to May Co. in 1946, kept the store alive until 2005, when May Co. was sold to Federated Department Stores Inc. and all of its remaining properties came under the Macy's brand. In the end, Kaufmann's and Saks were the last two standing in what once had been a thriving urban shopping scene.

One

BEGINNINGS

The founding generation of Kaufmann's Department Store is seen here in the 1890s along with their wives. From left to right are Jacob and Augusta, Henry and Theresa, Morris and Betty, and Isaac and Emma. Morris and Betty were the parents of Edgar J. Kaufmann, the longtime visionary chairman of the company. Isaac and Emma were the parents of Edgar's future wife, Lillian.

Jacob and Isaac Kaufmann opened the family's first store, J. Kaufmann & Bro., in 1871 at 1916 Carson Street in the town of Birmingham, now known as Pittsburgh's South Side. The single-floor shop specialized in men's clothing, particularly in suits custom-made by the Kaufmanns themselves. Brother Morris Kaufmann arrived from Germany in 1872, shortly after the brothers had moved to a slightly larger store at 1932 Carson Street.

In 1875, the Kaufmann brothers opened a branch store in Allegheny City, now Pittsburgh's North Side. They soon closed both that store and their Carson Street shop in favor of a larger store in downtown Pittsburgh. By this time, brother Isaac had immigrated and joined the business, now known as Kaufmann's Cheapest Corner. Opened in 1879, the new four-story building sat at the corner of modern-day Forbes Avenue (then known as Diamond Alley) and Smithfield Street. In 1882, a grand staircase and "electric burners" (electric lights) were installed, the first steps of many to modernize Kaufmann's.

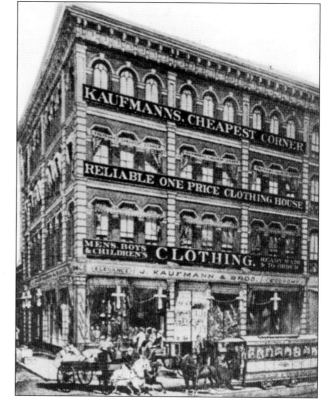

Once the Kaufmann brothers had a foothold on a major downtown Pittsburgh thoroughfare, their store began to grow down the block of Smithfield Street toward Fifth Avenue. This c. 1883 advertisement shows that J. Kaufmann & Bro. occupied 83, 85, and 87 Smithfield Street.

In 1885, the Kaufmann brothers began construction on a new store at the corner of Smithfield Street and Fifth Avenue. This building became known as Kaufmann's Grand Depot and cost $60,000 to build. It opened in 1885 to great fanfare and, in 1886, the company added women's clothing to its offerings.

Kaufmann's Grand Depot truly lived up to its name with its dramatic turret on the corner of Smithfield Street and Fifth Avenue, topped by a statue of the allegorical figure Liberty, her torch lighted by natural gas.

Main Aisle from Smithfield Street Entrance.

This late 1880s advertising piece shows the first-floor interior of the Grand Depot from the Smithfield Street entrance. This store had electricity from its opening day, a necessity with such a large area to light. Daylight from the building's large windows alone would not have sufficed.

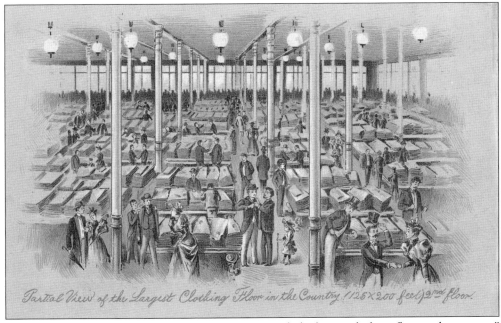

Partial View of the Largest Clothing Floor in the Country (125 X 200 feet) 2nd floor.

The reverse of the same advertising piece shows a view of "the largest clothing floor in the country," including measurements. The store also featured a large auto supply department that produced its own catalog in 1912, before auto supply shops became commonplace.

Compliments of

KAUFMANNS' GRAND DEPOT.

Fifth Avenue & Smithfield Street.

Between 1891 and 1913, Kaufmann's acquired the remainder of their block along both Smithfield Street and Fifth Avenue. In 1898, the company commissioned architect Charles Bickel to design a new expansion at the Forbes Avenue end of the block, to the right of the Grand Depot building. Bickel's building remains in place today.

These photographs, both taken on April 9, 1912, at the corner of Smithfield and Diamond Streets (formerly Diamond Alley and now Forbes Avenue), show the new building Charles Bickel designed for Kaufmann's. Note the Belle Epoque–style awning, reminiscent of the grand department stores of Europe. These entrances led to a hub of bargain shopping in what the company then called its Annex Shops. (Both, courtesy of the University of Pittsburgh Archives Service Center.)

This c. 1930s image shows the façade detail of the upper floors of the Charles Bickel building (right). The building at left was constructed in 1913 by the firm of Janssen & Abbott. Together, these two buildings occupied the entire block of Smithfield Street between Fifth and Forbes Avenues extending back to Cherry Way.

Two

THE MERCHANT PRINCE AND PRINCESS BUILD AN EMPIRE

Edgar Jonas Kaufmann (1885–1954), son of store cofounder Morris Kaufmann, became known in the popular press as "the merchant prince" due to his status as the heir to the business his father and uncles had built. E.J., as he was called, began working in the family business in 1909 as a shipping clerk and worked his way up to company president in 1913. That same year, after he and his father bought out the shares of seven co-owners, E.J. incorporated the business as Kaufmann Department Stores Inc.

Lillian Kaufmann (1889–1952) was the only daughter of Kaufmann's cofounder Isaac Kaufmann. She married her first cousin E.J. Kaufmann in 1909, consolidating much of the extended family's company shares into one partnership. She was the "merchant princess" to E.J.'s merchant prince and showed a certain panache for upscale shopping, scouring Europe for the best designs in fashion, decorative goods, and display ideas for her personally curated department, the Vendôme Shop. Consistent with her devotion to the finer things in life, she changed the spelling and pronunciation of her name to "Liliane" as an adult. The couple's only child, Edgar J. Kaufmann Jr., was born in 1910. (Courtesy of the Western Pennsylvania Conservancy.)

In 1913, E.J. Kaufmann commissioned the firm of Janssen & Abbott to design a new building to replace the Grand Depot. This structure would more closely match the aesthetic of the 1898 Charles Bickel design, with a façade of white terra cotta tiles rather than the brownstone of the Grand Depot. Collectively, these two buildings became known as "the Big Store." (Author's collection.)

This 1914 image shows an advertisement for the Big Store on the side of a building on Second Avenue downtown, about three blocks from Kaufmann's. (Courtesy of the University of Pittsburgh Archives Service Center.)

As both the staff of Kaufmann's and its number of departments grew, cofounder Henry Kaufmann came up with a way to easily communicate with all employees: The *Storagram* newsletter began in 1919 and was published continuously through 2006. Initially, the store had a team of reporters, seen here in the 1920s, who were tasked with writing stories about new store features and staff updates. The photographs taken for this purpose provide a rich archive of the company's operations over the decades.

E.J. Kaufmann was not only a retail genius, but also a connoisseur of the arts and champion of technology. His tenure as company president saw the store begin a series of cultural expositions, exhibitions, and contests meant to make the store a purveyor of more than just merchandise and to bring culture to the masses who may not have had the means to travel. The International Exposition of Arts and Industries took place in the early 1920s and was among the earliest of E.J. Kaufmann's cultural forays. Here is a view of the store's first floor during the exposition.

Each booth in the International Exposition of Arts and Industries featured a different country's displays of technology, craft, and arts. The United States' booth was on one of the store's upper floors, where it displayed some of its most cutting-edge technology, including handheld Kodak motion picture cameras.

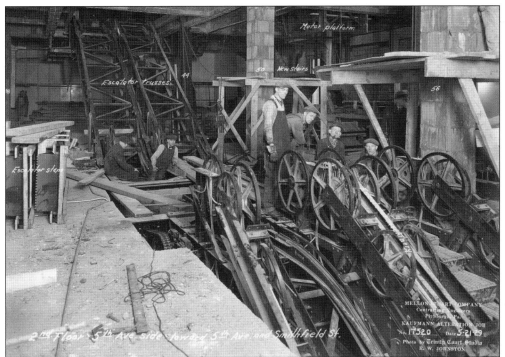

Kaufmann's was continuously updating its infrastructure, first installing escalators in 1924. This spring 1929 photograph shows the installation of a new escalator system, which the company claimed to be "the largest escalator system in the United States." The new system doubled the store's original capacity, accommodating over one-and-a-half-million shoppers each day. These 1929 images show the installation of two different banks of escalators on the second floor of the Big Store. The set above took customers to the Fifth Avenue and Smithfield Street side of the building. The set below went to the opposite side of the building, at Diamond Street (later Forbes Avenue) and Smithfield Street.

As department stores across the country sought to become one-stop shops, they expanded beyond typical merchandise to encroach on the territory of druggists and even grocers. This 1920s image shows a prescription department on the first floor.

No doubt banking on the ability of new-fangled gadgets to get customers into the store, Kaufmann's placed its selection of cameras next to its automobile supply department. Car parts stores were rare at that time.

One department essential to the Big Store's female customer was millinery, seen here in 1923. This department had both a ready-to-wear section and this one, which Kaufmann's referred to as the Adoria room. Here, clerks would help customers select and customize their hats. The word "Adoria" was also used for the company's salons.

Menswear was Kaufmann's first product and always one of its most important. This newspaper ad from September 1923 advertises men's hats for autumn. (Courtesy of *Pittsburgh Post-Gazette* archives.)

The women's suits department is pictured here in 1925. Shopping at a department store in this period was truly a full-service experience. Customers had the full attention of a clerk, who would show them merchandise, have them fitted, and then process the sale.

Kaufmann's prided itself on not only stocking merchandise for day-to-day needs, but also goods for special occasions, as seen in this 1931 ad for ready-to-wear Halloween costumes. (Courtesy of *Pittsburgh Post-Gazette* archives.)

In 1924, E.J. Kaufmann returned to his friend Benno Janssen of the architectural firms Janssen & Abbott and Janssen & Cocken to design a private home for his family in the Pittsburgh suburb of Fox Chapel. The result, named "La Tourelle," took its inspiration from a Norman castle—perhaps fitting for "retail royalty." The Kaufmanns sold the home in the early 1930s; it is now privately owned. (Author's collection.)

In 1925, E.J. Kaufmann's connoisseurship of art and architecture led him to orchestrate a massive modernization of the flagship store's main selling floor. Kaufmann once again turned to Benno Janssen to oversee the work through his new firm, Janssen & Cocken. The work was completed in 1930.

Janssen & Cocken's renovation turned what had been a functional, though staid, selling floor into an Art Deco showplace. The white plaster pillars with wooden wainscoting were dramatically transformed by their new covering of black Carrara glass. The upper portion of each column, as well as each beam extending across the ceiling, was covered in a custom-blown glass that diffused the glow of electric lights beneath.

This photograph shows in dramatic detail how the electric lights shone through the custom-blown glass to create an ambient light effect. The background shows portions of *The History of Commerce*, an art installation by Boardman Robinson commissioned as part of the first-floor renovation.

The addition of Boardman Robinson's murals to the first floor created stunning vistas from the Arcade level and various escalators leading to the main floor. New, custom-made fixtures for the first floor were crafted out of blond mahogany and set in a diagonal pattern rather than in straight squares.

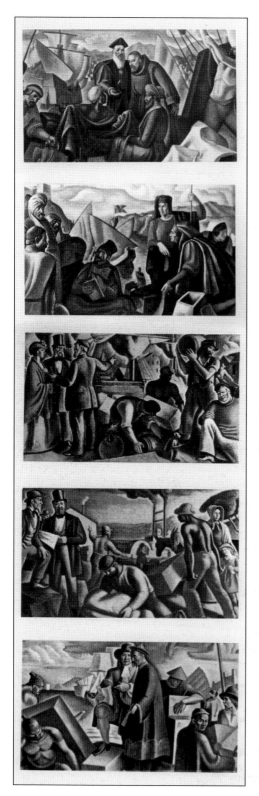

Boardman Robinson (1876–1952) was a Canadian artist best known for his cartoons and illustrations. He was commissioned to paint a series of murals for Kaufmann's titled *The History of Commerce* in 1929. The 10-panel series was mounted along the frieze around the perimeter of the store's main selling floor. The works highlighted important milestones in the history of trade from the ancient to the modern, including *The Carthaginians in the Mediterranean*; *The English in China*; and *Trade and Commerce, 20th Century*. The murals were removed in the 1950s and placed in the custody of the Pittsburgh History and Landmarks Foundation, which sold them to the Arts Center in Colorado Springs in the 1990s.

Janssen & Cocken's renovations were not confined to the store's interior; Kaufmann's ornate Belle Epoque entrances were modified to include sleek flat metal awnings with recessed lighting.

This c. 1930s image of women's blouses on the first floor shows some of the decorative metalwork that was installed during the remodeling. Behind the metalwork is the Arcade level.

No detail was left untouched during the renovation. Fixtures such as drinking fountains (left) and elevator doors (below) were also redesigned in highly stylized Art Deco. While many of the elements of the 1930 renovation were later dismantled, these two elements remained until the store's final days. (Author's collection.)

KAUFMANN'S SUMMER CAMP

BEAR RUN PA.

Page Seventeen

In 1916, shortly after E.J. Kaufmann became president of the store, he secured a lease on a parcel of land around Pennsylvania Route 381 that was then owned by a group of Masons. He operated the land as a summer camp for Kaufmann's employees, eventually buying the land outright in 1927. The *Storagram* employee newsletter published many photographs of employees frolicking in and around Bear Run, a stream flowing through the area. Around 1930, the camp was closed, and the Kaufmanns began to make plans for private use of the land.

In the mid-1930s, E.J. Kaufmann commissioned architect Frank Lloyd Wright to build a home on the family's property at Bear Run, in Pennsylvania's Laurel Highlands. The home represents a rare synergy between architect and client, as Kaufmann was one of the few able to work successfully with the cantankerous Wright. The Fallingwater commission marked a revitalization of Wright's career, which in recent years had declined. The house, now open to the public, is known worldwide as Wright's most famous work. (Courtesy of the Western Pennsylvania Conservancy.)

After Frank Lloyd Wright had designed Fallingwater for his family, E.J. Kaufmann commissioned the architect to design him a new office to replace his old one in the northwest corner of the flagship store's 10th floor. As was typical of Wright, he designed not only the room but also the furniture and light fixtures. In 1973, E.J.'s son, who had preserved the room after his father's death, donated the entire office interior to the Victoria & Albert Museum in London. It is the only Wright design in Europe. (Courtesy Western Pennsylvania Conservancy.)

Three

MEET ME UNDER THE CLOCK

In 1913, Kaufmann's installed an enormous clock above the corner of Fifth Avenue and Smithfield Street. Manufactured by the Coldwell Clock Company in New York, it weighs 2,500 pounds, though many of its decorative fittings are hollow. Though beloved by generations of Pittsburghers as a popular meeting place and universal symbol of the store, this was not the first Kaufmann's clock.

The original Kaufmann's clock (seen here at far right) was installed outside the Grand Depot shortly after the building opened in 1886. Set on a pedestal, the clock featured a sign hanging beneath its four faces that read, "Meet me under the clock." Thus, one of Pittsburgh's great traditions was born.

This image shows the clock (right) in 1912, shortly before it was removed during the demolition of the Grand Depot building. (Courtesy University of Pittsburgh Archives Service Center.)

At the time the Big Store building was erected in 1913, the store owners had not intended to replace the original clock. An internal company history notes that "letters, telephone calls and requests made over the counter were so numerous that the clock was set in its accustomed place, where it watches over the thousands that pass daily." Here, a lunchtime crowd passes under the clock in 1937. In terms of marketing, replacing the original clock was genius. It provided an instantly recognizable, easily marketed symbol of the store for over a century.

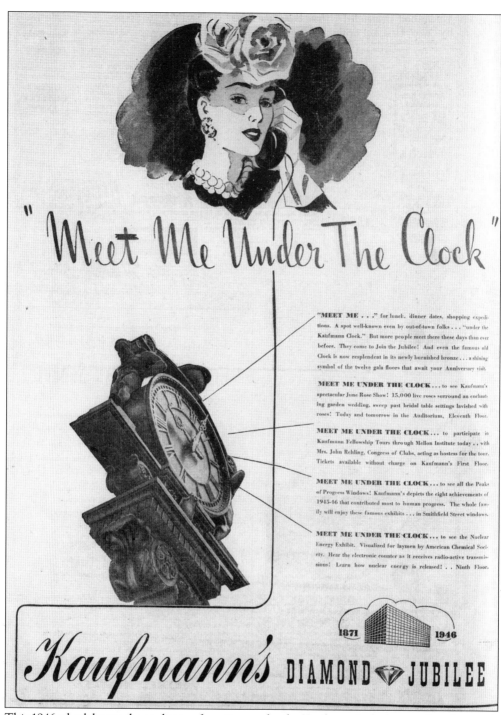

This 1946 ad celebrates the tradition of meeting under the Kaufmann's clock, as well as the store's diamond jubilee anniversary. (Courtesy of *Pittsburgh Post-Gazette* archives.)

In 1987, the Kaufmann's clock underwent a much-needed complete restoration. After spending eight decades in one of the dirtiest parts of the city, the once-shiny brass clock was dingy with soot and grime, and the works needed repairs. Architectural Artifacts Inc. was the firm contracted to do the work. They dismantled the entire clock and painstakingly restored each component, blasting the pieces with over 1,000 pounds of ground corncobs, which would not damage the brass itself. It took 10 weeks to restore the clock, and one month just to clean the brass. Above, workers compare a restored clock figure with its twin that awaits cleaning. The figures themselves are hollow. During restoration, the clock got new inner workings along with new hands and scrollwork.

Those few Pittsburghers who do not immediately recognize artist Linda Barnicott's name are sure to recognize her iconic images of Pittsburgh's landmarks, especially the Kaufmann's clock. Her first painting of the subject, titled *Meet Me Under the Kaufmann's Clock*, was completed in 1989. Barnicott credits Kaufmann's with starting her career, as prints of the painting were highly sought after, making her a household name in the area. (Courtesy of Linda Barnicott.)

Meet Me Under Kaufmann's Clock Too was released in 1993 after Barnicott received many requests for the now sold-out print of her original painting. (Courtesy of Linda Barnicott.)

In what eventually became a series of five paintings, Linda Barnicott continued to paint different views of the Kaufmann's clock over the years, emphasizing the nostalgia of the downtown shopping experience free from the distractions of advertisements of neighboring stores and road congestion. *Waiting for You Under Kaufmann's Clock* was painted as a fundraiser for the American Cancer Society in 2002. (Courtesy of Linda Barnicott.)

Barnicott's 2011 painting, *Holiday Memories Under Kaufmann's Clock*, was another fundraiser piece done for Breathe Pennsylvania. Barnicott's series inadvertently documented the last decades of the store's tenure as Kaufmann's as well as several after its conversion to Macy's in 2006. (Courtesy of Linda Barnicott.)

The newly-restored clock was unveiled by Pittsburgh mayor Richard Caligiuri (center) as part of the 1987 Light-Up Night festivities. Here, he poses after revealing the clock to the public.

The face of the Kaufmann's clock is lighted so it can be seen at night. On August 12, 2008, Pittsburgh mayor Luke Ravenstahl held a ceremony under the clock to name the corner of Fifth Avenue and Smithfield Street "Kaufmann Way." The ceremonial street sign remains.

Four

AFTER THE
MERCHANT PRINCE

E.J. Kaufmann died on April 14, 1955, and his passing inspired a wave of grief throughout Western Pennsylvania and beyond. In his honor, the flagship store was closed on April 19, the date of his funeral at Temple Rodef Shalom in Pittsburgh's Oakland neighborhood. Kaufmann's local competitors—Frank & Seder, Gimbels, Horne's and Rosebaum's—paid tribute to E.J. with an advertisement published in all of the city's daily newspapers. (Courtesy of the *Pittsburgh Post-Gazette* archives.)

Within a year of E.J. Kaufmann's death, the new management gave the flagship store yet another makeover. The first floor's Art Deco black glass and marble columns were covered over with plywood and painted white. As the years progressed, more and more of the fixtures from the 1930s remodeling were removed or covered over.

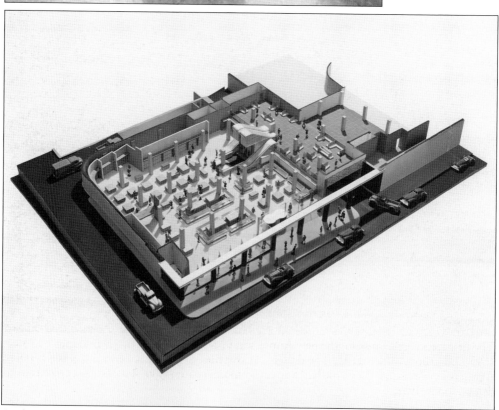

At the time of E.J.'s death, Kaufmann's had been busy constructing a building that would become known as the Annex along the Fifth Avenue side of the store's property. This architectural rendering shows Fifth Avenue to the right.

The first construction task for the new Annex was to demolish the Carnegie Building, a 13-story 1895 Longfellow, Alden & Harlow design. At the time of its construction, it was the tallest skyscraper in Pittsburgh. Here, the building's magnificent central spiral staircase sits exposed during demolition in 1952.

The main store buildings remained open during Annex construction. As there was a street—Cherry Way—between the blocks occupied by the Kaufmann's (background) and Carnegie (foreground) buildings, an underpass had to be built into the new design.

This view of Fifth Avenue in 1954 shows the steel skeleton of Kaufmann's Annex rising above Cherry Way.

Note the Annex building's lack of windows, no longer needed in a building with robust electric capabilities. The Annex was fully air-conditioned, a feature sure to get customers into the store on hot summer days.

This 1955 view of Fifth Avenue shows the Annex façade with its sleek granite pillars.

The familiar circled "K" logo was introduced along with the Annex itself. The company used it through the 1970s.

The opening celebration for Kaufmann's Annex took place in the spring of 1955. Above, store management, employees, and VIPs celebrate with a logo-topped cake. Below, ladies dressed in 1871 fashions circulate through the crowd, commemorating the year the company was founded.

Five

EVERYTHING UNDER THE SUN

First Floor on opening day found business brisk and Anniversary interest high.

Kaufmann's always made a big deal about its anniversary. The store celebrated each June, "the month of roses," with its biggest sale of the year. In addition to the sale, June always brought new interior décor and fresh window displays for shoppers.

Kaufmann's Annex Sets Sail for Its Second Successful Year's Cruise

The first year a huge success, leaving every promise of a similarly successful one to come . . . such was the lot of this store for men that specializes in low-priced clothing. Every Kaufmann charge account is honored here . . . the regular Kaufmann delivery force is at the service of Annex customers and typically Kaufmann courtesy is ever available.

"Plus-Six" Suits and Overcoats of Fine Quality

Made exclusively for the "Annex" and having more than their quota of quality-for-price, "Plus Six" suits and overcoats represent the best 21.50 values in town. Assortments are ever full, variety is always satisfactorily large and the fabrics are all made by well known makers. Every man's size is here in this winter display.

Plus-Six Topcoats Plus-Six Tuxedos
21.50 21.50

KAUFMANN'S ANNEX

TWO ENTRANCES   406 DIAMOND ST.
114 SMITHFIELD ST.

"Left-Over Days" were Kaufmann's version of Filene's Basement, which May Co., Kaufmann's parent company, later came to own. Hundreds of shoppers would crowd into the basement of the store to hunt for steeply discounted treasures, as seen in this c. 1959 photograph.

Before the large Annex building was built in 1955, Kaufmann's had sections of the store it called Annex Shops, with entrances at Smithfield Street and what is now Forbes Avenue. Rather than featuring unsold merchandise at a discount, these shops offered lower-priced clothing brands. The Annex Shops lasted from 1926 to 1955. (Courtesy of *Pittsburgh Post-Gazette* archives.)

50

Kaufmann's Downstairs was yet another bargain department that existed throughout many of the store's iterations. This department offered a mix of discounted, unsold merchandise as well as lower-priced brands. Also known as "Kaufmann's Basement," the department closed several decades before the flagship store's demise. This ad is from 1955. (Courtesy of *Pittsburgh Post-Gazette* archives.)

The Annex allowed Kaufmann's to expand its children's departments, an important improvement during the height of the baby boom. These 1955 photographs show the updated baby department (above)—with comfortable seating for mom as she chooses baby's many layette sets—and the toddler girls' department (below) with its low display fixtures allowing little ones to shop along with mother. A maternity department made its debut on the fifth floor the same year.

While Kaufmann's had always carried menswear, in the 1950s, it began to specifically court a new crowd: college-bound teenagers. There were college shops for both men and women. In 1955, the store featured sports cars in its windows to advertise the opening of its College Shop.

Kaufmann's College Shop Opens and Windows Feature Sports Cars

. . . Fourth Floor College Shop abounds in exciting campus clothes . . .

Menswear departments in the new Annex included the Clay Poole shop, featuring ready-to-wear men's suits that could be quickly tailored, as well as a newly-outfitted shoe department. Kaufmann's always had full-service shoe departments, with salespeople working on commission.

The extra space created in the Annex allowed Kaufmann's to turn the fifth floor into a womenswear paradise. As the Annex opened in the spring of 1955, the initial inventory was all spring and summer wares. Above are women's summer party dresses; below is the women's shoe department.

The new construction was an opportunity to update all the store's fixtures. The women's millinery department featured new desk-like furniture designed especially for hat sales. The customer would sit in the seat with a mirror directly facing her while the clerk brought hats to try.

The Vendôme Shop was the brainchild of Liliane Kaufmann. She served as the main buyer for this department for many years, traveling in person to Europe to select merchandise and shipping it back. In addition to upscale women's clothing, the Vendôme Shop also carried a selection of accessories such as hats, handbags, scarves, and footwear (above). The shop occasionally hosted trunk shows for popular designers of the day. Upscale departments like this would have models come out to show clothing, which customers could then opt to try on (below).

Customers browse the new housewares departments, including silverware and electric appliances, in 1955.

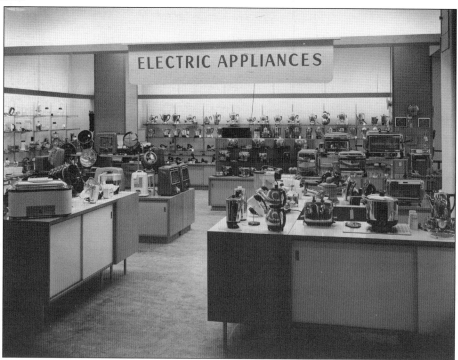

Kaufmann's invested heavily in the comfort of its customers with the Annex expansion. Here, the linens department offers many chairs for buyers to use while selecting fabrics.

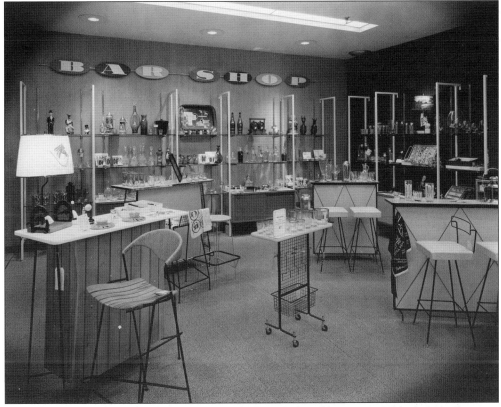

The focus of Kaufmann's departments shifted along with public tastes. With the popularity in the 1960s of bars in the home and office, the store featured a Bar Shop.

The furniture departments in the expanded building were upgraded to allow for mini-galleries showing multiple rooms' worth of furniture in a smaller amount of space. The store offered a full complement of furnishings, including pianos, cabinet turntables, and sewing machines.

While more associated today with suburban megastores, Kaufmann's flagship store did sell hardware at one point. The store had long dabbled in do-it-yourself type departments, such as auto supplies and gardening implements, as seen on the following page.

Kaufmann's had patio shops at all of its stores, including the suburban locations. The flagship's patio shop operated until the early 1990s.

Kaufmann's book department once occupied space on the main selling floor. Departments were frequently moved around over the years; eventually, this department was moved to the upper floors of the store.

The Carnegie Library of Pittsburgh's Downtown & Business branch found a home in Kaufmann's Annex in 1957. The store united for the first time the Business branch, formerly located on Oliver Avenue, and the Downtown branch, which had been housed in the Frick Building for a time. Though this home was a temporary one, it doubled the amount of book space the two separate branches had previously had. The branch now has a permanent home at 612 Smithfield Street.

One of the odder departments on offer at Kaufmann's was the surgical supplies department on the first floor. Two specially trained technicians, one male and one female, were available to discuss customers' medical needs and to fit them for anything from surgical stockings to hearing aids. The department also rented and sold wheelchairs.

Epicure Shop Opens On Seventh Floor

Kaufmann's newly enlarged Epicure Shop is a delight for all gourmets. Fabulous delicacies, as well as a freezing unit well-stocked with familiar favorites, are arranged in appetizing array.

The Epicure Shop opened on Kaufmann's seventh floor in 1955. This was actually not the store's only attempt at selling groceries; it first carried foodstuffs in 1890. The grocery department was phased out in the early 1920s, as the company acknowledged it was better at selling other types of items. However, gourmet foods such as fine chocolates were always on offer, in addition to the store's in-house bakery and restaurants.

This April 1979 ad touts the introduction of Kaufmann's new Pirate shop on the third floor. The store introduced its own trademarked "Bad Bandana" as a counterpart to the Steelers' "Terrible Towel." The Pirates went on to win that year's World Series. (Courtesy of *Pittsburgh Post-Gazette* archives.)

The women's accessories department, seen here in the 1990s, shows the continued evolution of Kaufmann's first floor with mirrored pillars and carpeting.

More views of the main selling floor in the 1990s are seen here, with women's clothing and the cosmetics/fragrance counters.

Six

WINDOW SHOPPING

The Big Store included a double window at the corner of Fifth Avenue and Smithfield Street. This was where Kaufmann's placed all its show-stopping displays, especially at Christmastime. This c. 1923 anniversary display shows fashions of 1871, a frequent subject as it was the year the company was founded.

LOOK IN OUR WINDOW

AND YOU HAVE THE PROOFS!

Yes, cast your optics through the pure and true crystal plates of our Mammoth Corner Window and there see for yourself the evidence of the truth of all we say and claim for our Great House Cleaning Sale. See the various samples of the Bargains to be found inside. There is nothing to confuse, but everything is made plain and easy for the prospective buyer. Each garment is marked in plain figures what it is to be sold for, and—mind you!—you won't hear such remarks as: "That's the last one in the window," or, "We haven't your size," etc. We want you to know and feel that, though the entire city may fairly ring with fictitious sales and bold bluffs of unscrupulous clothiers, OURS IS A GENUINE, BONA-FIDE REDUCTION SALE, and this advertisement an HONEST, STRAIGHTFORWARD STATEMENT OF FACTS, proved such by the figures (price marks) in our window and the qualities you are asked to examine. Wish that every purchaser were an expert on Clothing, or, if he is not, would bring one with him. It would greatly facilitate the work for our salesmen.

See the Men's Fine Suits in Kaufmanns' Corner Window,

MARKED $10, $12 AND $15!

They're Bargains in all the word implies; nothing offered elsewhere can approach them with a 40-foot pole. Kaufmanns' have never given bigger and fuller value than they give right now. The Suits marked $10 cannot be duplicated elsewhere below $16, $17 and $18; those which you see in Kaufmanns' window marked $12 are other dealers' regular $20, $21 and $23 Suits, while those on which the price ticket says $15, are held by the trade at from $25 to $30.

See the Sample Pants in Kaufmanns' Corner Window,

MARKED $2.00, $3.00, $3.50, $4.00, $5.00 AND $6.00!

Each pair is worth double the price—NEARLY. If you want a pair Pants, here is your chance. Don't be backward about coming in and examining the qualities. You'll please us by so doing, and don't incur the slightest obligation to buy. Unless you see, feel and decide for yourself that any pair of Pants you may choose is a Grand Bargain, we would rather have you not patronize us. We want our Bargains to go to people who can appreciate them.

See the Boys' Fine Suits in Kaufmanns' Corner Window,

MARKED $3 AND $5, AND WORTH FROM $5 TO $9!

Parents, you who have Boys to clothe, don't ignore this offer. Your Boys may be well supplied at present—but what's the matter with the future? You can get the goods now for half the money you'll have to pay for them two or three months hence. Wouldn't it be a good investment, then, to purchase now? Many of the Suits are just the right thing for Boys' Spring wear—in style, in weight, in pattern. Be wise and don't delay a single day, but come at once.

The Latest Styles of Spring Overcoats Are Here Now!

And Sample Garments can be seen displayed in our Corner Window. They are nothing if not perfection. Ready-made in name; Custom-made in fact. Stylish-dressing Gentlemen, look at these goods before you leave your measure. The prices are most reasonable.

KAUFMANNS'

GRAND DEPOT

Fifth Avenue and Smithfield Street.

Like the Big Store after it, Kaufmann's Grand Depot also featured a large window at the corner of Fifth Avenue and Smithfield Street. This 1888 advertisement touts a display of men's and boy's clothing in its largest window. (Courtesy of *Pittsburgh Post-Gazette* archives.)

Kaufmann's anniversary month of June was always advertised as "the month of roses," and much of the décor and advertising reflected that theme, as seen here in an 81st anniversary window from 1952.

Kaufmann's planned elaborate displays each year to celebrate its anniversary in June. This image from the early 1920s shows a diorama of Pres. Grover Cleveland's wedding, part of that year's theme of "Moments in History."

KAUFMANN'S DRAMATIZES "PEAKS OF PROGRESS"
and salutes Jet Propulsion as one of the nine great achievements of the year

For ten years now, Kaufmann's Peaks of Progress windows have dramatized the achievements of the year, most important to the progress of mankind. Famous throughout America, their contribution to the recording of America's progress is vitally significant. Chosen by a committee of eminent Pittsburghers, these windows are created by our own Display Studios. We are proud to have chosen this means of marking Kaufmann's progress through 74 years.

OFFICIAL NAVY PHOTOGRAPH
Grumman "Avenger," assisted by jet units, swept into air in less than half its normal take-off run.

See Jet Propulsion, revolutionary development in man's conquest of the air, and eight other Peaks of Progress portrayed today and every day during June in Kaufmann's own windows along Smithfield Street.

JET PROPULSION ADVANCES AVIATION

SEE WAR DIORAMAS in our Twelfth Floor Auditorium every day during June! Exciting, huge, three-dimensional models of American boys in action from Tunisia to Alaska. Breath-taking scenes, in full color, show how our boys live and fight. No charge for admission!

The Peaks of Progress was another of Kaufmann's many ongoing exhibits. For decades, store executives including E.J. Kaufmann would decide on a series of technological innovations to highlight in the store's windows. Each year had a theme, sometimes focusing on important technological developments of the past or present. This ad from June 1945 shows a window celebrating advances in aviation. (Courtesy of *Pittsburgh Post-Gazette* archives.)

Oliver Kaufmann, one of E.J. Kaufmann's cousins, kept a personal photographic record of many of the store's windows from the 1920s and 1930s. Above is a selection of men's golf wear. Below, baby grand pianos are seen in what must have been quite a spacious window. Both images are from the late 1920s.

Kaufmann's windows were always reflective of not only the current fashions, but also current events. During World War II, the store's windows advertised its participation in the war effort. A Victory Center was established on the first floor, with a counter for buying war bonds and posting parcels to men and women serving overseas.

This 1940s window display of writing implements encouraged those on the home front to write letters to their servicemen and women.

Kaufmann's even paid tribute to the women entering the workforce in support of the war effort with this c. 1942 window.

This 1940s window advertised naval recruitment sessions taking place inside the store's Victory Center. The company's *Storagram* newsletter notified employees of wartime deaths during all of the United States' armed conflicts.

Window shoppers cluster around a c. 1950 window display proclaiming, "Television is here / Linking us by coaxial cable with top New York television stations / See for yourself / Radio Department, Seventh Floor." (Courtesy of the University of Pittsburgh Archives Service Center.)

Outdoor displays were sometimes not limited to the windows. This 1950s springtime display features floral sprays sprouting from the store's awnings.

This c. 1976 image shows the covers that were placed over the 1930 metal awnings. Note the store hours banner: Kaufmann's did not open on Sundays until 1977, when some of Pennsylvania's blue laws were repealed.

While the Christmas season was the biggest draw for Kaufmann's windows, that didn't prevent the store from celebrating other holidays. These two windows from 2001 show houseware and clothing displays with a Halloween theme.

Seven

EVERY CONVENIENCE

A horse-drawn cart filled with parcels departs the Kaufmann's warehouse around 1890. Free delivery via horse-drawn wagon was introduced in 1884.

This fleet of Kaufmann's delivery boys rode penny-farthing bicycles in the late 1880s. The store asked customers to carry smaller parcels home themselves during busy months to ease the loads of its delivery men.

The rapid expansion of the store always meant more new technology. Kaufmann's debuted delivery trucks in the early 1930s.

The store's delivery fleet kept getting bigger and better. In the warehouse, workers would carefully pack household furniture such as vanities, breakfronts, and iceboxes for delivery.

In the late 1950s, Kaufmann's opened a parking garage directly across Forbes Avenue, which it operated under a long-term lease from the Pittsburgh Parking Authority. As a major new convenience for customers, the garage featured heavily in the store's advertising for decades.

A novel service for late 1950s parents, "tot-toters," today known as strollers, were made available to customers needing help getting their children and packages to the parking garage safely.

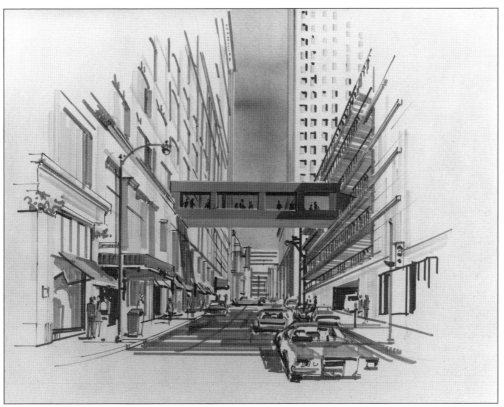

This architectural sketch shows the covered pedestrian walkway connecting the parking garage to the store's second floor. The bridge over Forbes Avenue was completed in 1987.

Kaufmann's began its portrait studio department in the 1890s and had the first department store photography studio in Pittsburgh. Later, offerings expanded to include developing of personal camera film.

In 1955, with the opening of the new Annex, the bridal shop was upgraded with antique furnishings and hand-painted murals. Here, a bride would find a one-stop shop for selecting a gown, registering for gifts, and even ordering a cake from Kaufmann's in-house bakery.

The fur department was an easy way to bring repeat customers to the store. Here, furs could not only be selected in a separate showroom, they could also be custom fitted and stored for the off-season.

Here, employees clean furs with sawdust. The specialized nature of caring for and storing furs kept customers loyal to the store for decades.

Here, employees Phil Ionadi (left) and Anthony Costa perform alterations on furs purchased in the store. Kaufmann's tailors were skilled at restyling—adding or removing fur pieces to refit the coat to the customer.

The staff of Kaufmann's original Adoria salon stands in the manicure room around 1923. After the Annex expansion in 1955, this popular salon was enlarged to accommodate even more customers.

vendôme beauty
Elizabeth Arden

Kaufmann's also had an Elizabeth Arden salon in the Vendôme Shop. Each salon in the store had a different clientele and pricing scheme.

The Quick Clip salon was added to Kaufmann's third floor in the 1990s. This salon featured walk-in service and lower prices than its other, higher-end salons. (Courtesy of *Pittsburgh Post-Gazette* archives.)

QUICK CLIP SALON
EXPERT WALK-IN BEAUTY SERVICE ON FOUR

STOP IN AND LET OUR STYLISTS CREATE A HAIR STYLE ESPECIALLY FOR YOU IN OUR DOWNTOWN PITTSBURGH QUICK CLIP SALON ON FOUR. Take advantage of our everyday low prices on skillful service. No appointment. First come - first served. You're next!

HAIRCUT AND SHAMPOO ..... 8.50   BLOW DRY OR SET 8.50
SHAMPOO AND HAIRCUT WITH SET OR BLOW DRY $17
PERMANENT WAVE WITH HAIRCUT, SET OR BLOW DRY 25.50
Slightly higher for longer hair.
Also available: relaxers and curls. Hair style shown by Linda Venneri Smith.
Quick Clip Salon, Downtown Pittsburgh only. D. 219.

KAUFMANN'S

Almost as soon as telephones became available to the public, Kaufmann's began a mail order service. Seen here in the 1940s, operators sit at long counters with copies of advertisements and catalogs, processing sales.

Due to its longevity, Kaufmann's used many different methods of extending credit to its customers over the decades. Among the first methods used were metal charge fobs (above), which could be attached to a keyring or watch chain. They were engraved on the front with the Kaufmann's logo and had the customer's account number on the back. The final method used, was, of course, credit cards (below).

A variety of Kaufmann's gift boxes shows different styles and patterns used over the years. These boxes all feature the last logo the company used, dating from the 1980s. May Co.'s properties generally used the same box styles, simply changing the name for each store.

Kaufmann's was home to many different restaurants over the years, the longest-lasting of which was the Tic Toc Restaurant. When it opened in 1956, it was known as the "Tic Toc Corner," since it was located in a corner of the store's first floor. The name and décor were inspired by Kaufmann's iconic clock. Many people also referred to it as the "Tic Toc Shop."

The Tic Toc Restaurant was redecorated many times over the years, but it always maintained the jovial air of a diner, serving quick eats like omelets, sandwiches, and other unfussy selections. Below is the Tic Toc as it looked shortly after it closed for good in 2015.

Kaufmann's *Storagram* newsletter made a point of highlighting every department at one time or another, introducing staff members and their jobs to their colleagues. Here, the newsletter celebrates the staff of the Arcade Tea Room, one of the store's many restaurants over the years.

Most of the store's restaurants were on the 10th and 11th floors. Many of these were more upscale, such as Michael's or the Forbes Room, while others added in later years showed a more casual vibe. Edgar's, for example, was opened in 1990 on the 10th floor, serving casual food in a fun atmosphere.

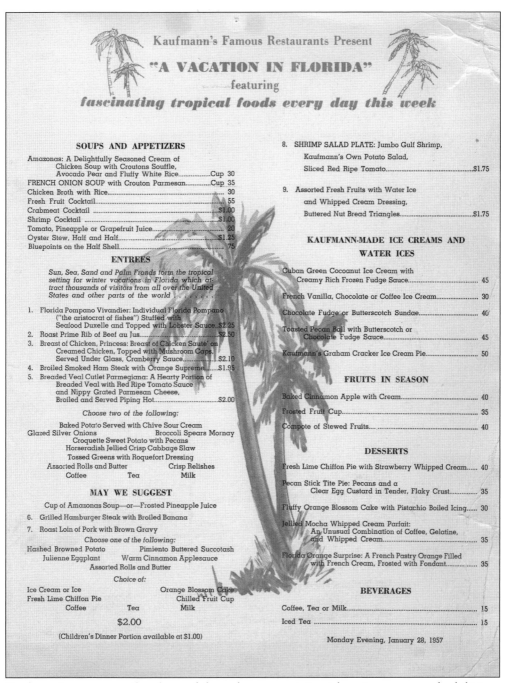

Kaufmann's Famous Restaurants Present

"A VACATION IN FLORIDA"

featuring

fascinating tropical foods every day this week

SOUPS AND APPETIZERS

Amazonas: A Delightfully Seasoned Cream of
   Chicken Soup with Croutons Souffle,
   Avocado Pear and Fluffy White Rice...............Cup 30
FRENCH ONION SOUP with Crouton Parmesan.............Cup 35
Chicken Broth with Rice.. 30
Fresh Fruit Cocktail... 55
Crabmeat Cocktail $1.00
Shrimp Cocktail $1.00
Tomato, Pineapple or Grapefruit Juice........................ 20
Oyster Stew, Half and Half.. $1.25
Bluepoints on the Half Shell.. 75

ENTREES

*Sun, Sea, Sand and Palm Fronds form the tropical
setting for winter vacations in Florida which at-
tract thousands of visitors from all over the United
States and other parts of the world . . . .*

1. Florida Pompano Vivandier: Individual Florida Pompano
   ("the aristocrat of fishes") Stuffed with
   Seafood Duxelle and Topped with Lobster Sauce..$2.25
2. Roast Prime Rib of Beef au Jus..................................$2.50
3. Breast of Chicken, Princess: Breast of Chicken Saute' on
   Creamed Chicken, Topped with Mushroom Caps,
   Served Under Glass, Cranberry Sauce.................$2.10
4. Broiled Smoked Ham Steak with Orange Supreme.......$1.95
5. Breaded Veal Cutlet Parmegiana: A Hearty Portion of
   Breaded Veal with Red Ripe Tomato Sauce
   and Nippy Grated Parmesan Cheese,
   Broiled and Served Piping Hot...............................$2.00

Choose two of the following:

Baked Potato Served with Chive Sour Cream
Glazed Silver Onions   Broccoli Spears Mornay
   Croquette Sweet Potato with Pecans
   Horseradish Jellied Crisp Cabbage Slaw
   Tossed Greens with Roquefort Dressing
Assorted Rolls and Butter   Crisp Relishes
   Coffee   Tea   Milk

MAY WE SUGGEST

Cup of Amazonas Soup—or—Frosted Pineapple Juice

6. Grilled Hamburger Steak with Broiled Banana
7. Roast Loin of Pork with Brown Gravy

Choose one of the following:

Hashed Browned Potato   Pimiento Buttered Succotash
   Julienne Eggplant   Warm Cinnamon Applesauce
   Assorted Rolls and Butter

Choice of:

Ice Cream or Ice   Orange Blossom Cake
Fresh Lime Chiffon Pie   Chilled Fruit Cup
   Coffee   Tea   Milk

$2.00

(Children's Dinner Portion available at $1.00)

8. SHRIMP SALAD PLATE: Jumbo Gulf Shrimp,
   Kaufmann's Own Potato Salad,
   Sliced Red Ripe Tomato...............................$1.75

9. Assorted Fresh Fruits with Water Ice
   and Whipped Cream Dressing,
   Buttered Nut Bread Triangles.......................$1.75

KAUFMANN-MADE ICE CREAMS AND WATER ICES

Cuban Green Cocoanut Ice Cream with
   Creamy Rich Frozen Fudge Sauce............................ 45

French Vanilla, Chocolate or Coffee Ice Cream.............. 30

Chocolate Fudge or Butterscotch Sundae...................... 40

Toasted Pecan Ball with Butterscotch or
   Chocolate Fudge Sauce... 45

Kaufmann's Graham Cracker Ice Cream Pie.................. 50

FRUITS IN SEASON

Baked Cinnamon Apple with Cream............................ 40

Frosted Fruit Cup.. 35

Compote of Stewed Fruits.. 40

DESSERTS

Fresh Lime Chiffon Pie with Strawberry Whipped Cream...... 40

Pecan Stick Tite Pie: Pecans and a
   Clear Egg Custard in Tender, Flaky Crust................. 35

Fluffy Orange Blossom Cake with Pistachio Boiled Icing...... 30

Jellied Mocha Whipped Cream Parfait:
   An Unusual Combination of Coffee, Gelatine,
   and Whipped Cream... 35

Florida Orange Surprise: A French Pastry Orange Filled
   with French Cream, Frosted with Fondant................. 35

BEVERAGES

Coffee, Tea or Milk.. 15

Iced Tea 15

Monday Evening, January 28, 1957

Kaufmann's restaurants often featured themed menus to tie in with various events and exhibitions happening in the store. During international celebrations, the restaurants would feature entire menus of French, Spanish, or Italian cuisine. This Floridian menu dates from 1957.

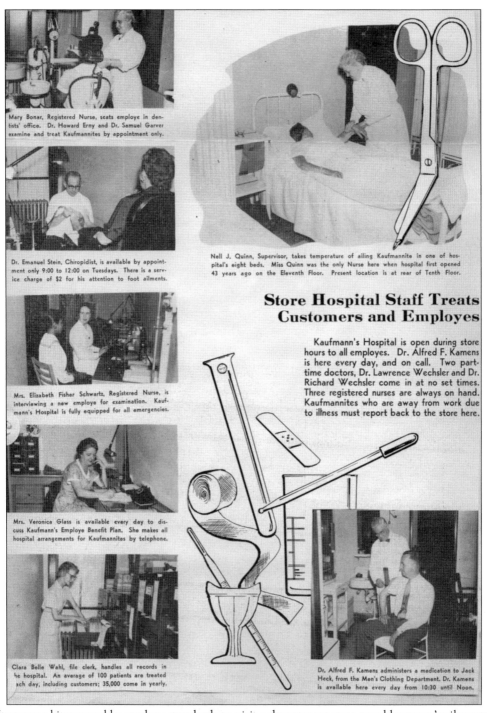

Mary Bonar, Registered Nurse, seats employe in dentists' office. Dr. Howard Erny and Dr. Samuel Garver examine and treat Kaufmannites by appointment only.

Dr. Emanuel Stein, Chiropidist, is available by appointment only 9:00 to 12:00 on Tuesdays. There is a service charge of $2 for his attention to foot ailments.

Mrs. Elizabeth Fisher Schwartz, Registered Nurse, is interviewing a new employe for examination. Kaufmann's Hospital is fully equipped for all emergencies.

Mrs. Veronica Glass is available every day to discuss Kaufmann's Employe Benefit Plan. She makes all hospital arrangements for Kaufmannites by telephone.

Clara Belle Wahl, file clerk, handles all records in he hospital. An average of 100 patients are treated ach day, including customers; 35,000 come in yearly.

Nell J. Quinn, Supervisor, takes temperature of ailing Kaufmannite in one of hospital's eight beds. Miss Quinn was the only Nurse here when hospital first opened 43 years ago on the Eleventh Floor. Present location is at rear of Tenth Floor.

Store Hospital Staff Treats Customers and Employes

Kaufmann's Hospital is open during store hours to all employes. Dr. Alfred F. Kamens is here every day, and on call. Two part-time doctors, Dr. Lawrence Wechsler and Dr. Richard Wechsler come in at no set times. Three registered nurses are always on hand. Kaufmannites who are away from work due to illness must report back to the store here.

Dr. Alfred F. Kamens administers a medication to Jack Heck, from the Men's Clothing Department. Dr. Kamens is available here every day from 10:30 until Noon.

It seems a bit unusual by modern standards to visit a department store to address one's ailments, but that's exactly what many Pittsburghers did at Kaufmann's. The store housed a hospital for decades. Every Kaufmann's employee was given a complete checkup upon employment and was entitled to visit the department for any health needs. The hospital was also open to the public and included eye and dental treatment in addition to first aid.

Eight

FOR EVERYTHING UNDER THE TREE

Pictured here is a true Christmas window at Kaufmann's in the late 1920s. The store's Christmas displays became more secular over time.

Though mass marketing to children is thought of as a more modern development, Kaufmann's was at it from its earliest days in downtown Pittsburgh. The *Kaufmann's Sunday School Greeting* was a booklet distributed to local schoolchildren in an effort to encourage them to bring their parents to shop at the store. The booklets had different themes each year, sometimes containing snippets of Dickens, Shakespeare, or even travelogues of far-off places.

Kaufmann's Big Store building had a crowd-pleasing feature: a large corner window on its Fifth Avenue and Smithfield Street side. For many years, this was the only window to contain mechanical elements, which were hand-operated by an employee stationed in a basement department. The staff would work in 30-minute shifts turning a crank to operate the displays. This c. 1930 Christmas display features Barney Google and his horse, Spark Plug, from the popular comic strip *Barney Google and Snuffy Smith*, which debuted in 1919 and later appeared as an animated short.

Each year's Christmas windows adopted a different theme. This one from the 1920s was part of a series of storybook dioramas. Here we see the tea party scene from Lewis Carroll's *Alice's Adventures in Wonderland*. Literary themes were popular; in 1890, an ad in the *Pittsburgh Daily Post* read, "If Shakespeare could look into Kaufmanns' [sic] corner window and there see his famous 'Seven Ages' illustrated by moving wax figures, how the bard would smile! Shakespeare can't see it—you can. Don't miss it."

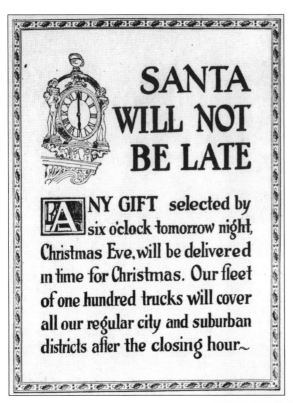

SANTA WILL NOT BE LATE

ANY GIFT selected by six o'clock tomorrow night, Christmas Eve, will be delivered in time for Christmas. Our fleet of one hundred trucks will cover all our regular city and suburban districts after the closing hour.

This advertisement from December 23, 1925, promises timely delivery of all purchases for Christmas. Much of the merchandise purchased by customers was later delivered to the home rather than carried out of the store.

Sometimes, the show-stopping displays were not in the windows at all. This 1930s display features an enormous urn full of candles atop one of the store's awnings.

Kaufmann's
Storagram

Published by
Kaufmann Employes
December, 1941

This copy of the Kaufmann's staff newsletter *Storagram* from December 1941 shows employees hard at work constructing an enormous elephant as part of the Toyland set where Santa would reside throughout the Christmas season.

Kaufmann's Christmas windows often reflected the changes in the country's—and particularly, their customers'—lives. These windows from the 1940s depict soldiers celebrating Christmas away from home.

Thousands of Pittsburgh's children flooded the ninth floor's Santaland each December to visit with Santa Claus. Charles "Teenie" Harris, a photographer for the *Pittsburgh Courier*, captured this scene of, from left to right, little Cathy, Kimberly, and Serena Blackman making their wishes known in 1966. (Courtesy of Teenie Harris Archives, Carnegie Museum of Art.)

Toyland Enlivens Our Ninth Floor

Kaufmann's Toyland — bigger than ever, better than ever and brimming over with fabulous gifts for small-fry — is a dream come true for thousands of youngsters now visiting the floor. Santa Claus is also on hand.

Toyland was a highlight of every December, truly "brimming with gifts for the small-fry," as it was billed. It was usually found on the ninth floor along with Santa.

Toy selections for girls and boys are seen here in 1949.

Like its future owner, Macy's, Kaufmann's used to sponsor a Thanksgiving Day Parade. This 1966 ad shows the parade route starting at the Civic Arena and moving toward Point State Park, passing the flagship store along Fifth Avenue.

This c. 1940s window shows Santa in his workshop with a message beseeching children to come visit him on the ninth floor in Toyland.

This window from the early 1950s was part of a series depicting old-fashioned Christmas celebrations. The placard reads, "Seventeen-thirty-seven is thought the first date / When a Christmas Eve party was planned for a fete. / The Lady of Wittenberg's children, all four, / Received tiny trees that they all could adore."

Kaufmann's offered different shopping experiences for the whole family. This 1961 ad lists upscale shops for adults, Trim-a-Home for décor, the Corner Shop for inexpensive gifts, and Toyland for children. (Courtesy of *Pittsburgh Post-Gazette* archives.)

This c. 1960 photograph shows the Kaufmann's Annex decorated for the Christmas season, with the large "K" logo lighted to look like an ornament.

These woodland Christmas windows were meant to show the five senses through which the forest critters are reminded of Christmas. Here, the bunny conductor leads the animals in a song around 1959.

Seen here are more scenes from the "Christmas in Woodland" theme. The message above reads, "Twas the night before Christmas and all through the woods / Every pixie was stirring as all pixies should. / Come near, Santa beckons with a wave of his hand, / 'See our forest folk windows then our ninth floor Toyland.' "

"CHRISTMAS AROUND THE WORLD"

featuring

a different national menu every day this week

It's "Noel" in France . .

SOUPS AND APPETIZERS

Petite Marmite	Cup 30
French Onion Soup with Crouton Parmesan	Cup 35
Chicken Broth with Rice	30
Fresh Fruit Cocktail	55
Crabmeat Cocktail	$1.00
Shrimp Cocktail	$1.00
Tomato, Pineapple or Grapefruit Juice	20
Oyster Stew, Half and Half	$1.25
Bluepoints on the Half Shell	75

ENTREES

*1. Roast Prime Rib of Beef au Jus $2.50
*2. Broiled African Lobster Tail with Drawn Butter $2.25
3. Roast Leg of Spring Lamb, Boulanger,
   Served with Parisienne Potatoes
   Mint Frosted Fresh Pineapple Ring $2.25
*4. Fresh Calves' Sweetbreads Saute' with
   Canadian Bacon, Marie Antoinette $2.00
*5. Broiled Ham Steak with Glazed Pineapple Ring,
   Bigarade Sauce $1.90

Choose two of the following:

Suzette Potato	Lyonnaise Potato
Broccoli Spears Hollandaise	Crisp Relishes
Jellied Cranberry Christmas Tree	
Iced Lettuce Hearts, Choice of Dressing	
Assorted Rolls and Butter	Crisp Relishes

Coffee   Tea   Milk

MAY WE SUGGEST

Cup of Petite Marmite Soup—or
Mint Frosted Fruit Nectar

6. Pan Fried Loin Pork Chop with Mushrooms, Forestier

7. Our Famous Chicken a la King:
   Big Chunks of Chicken in a Rich a la King Sauce
   Served with Toast Points

Choice of:

Pimiento Buttered Fordhook Lima Beans	
Julienne Eggplant	Warm Cinnamon Applesauce

Choice of:

Ice Cream or Ice	French Chocolate Cream Pie
Almond Cake	Chilled Fruit Cup

Coffee   Tea   Milk

$2.00

(Children's Dinner Portion available at $1.00)

8. Shrimp Salad Plate: Jumbo Gulf Shrimp,
   Kaufmann's Own Potato Salad,
   Sliced Red Ripe Tomato $1.75

9. Assorted Fresh Fruits with Water Ice
   and Whipped Cream Dressing,
   Buttered Nut Bread Triangles $1.75

**KAUFMANN-MADE ICE CREAMS AND
WATER ICES**

Lemon Drop Ice, Creme de Menthe	45
French Vanilla, Chocolate or Coffee Ice Cream	30
Chocolate Fudge or Butterscotch Sundae	40
French Coffee Ice Cream with Hot Bittersweet Sauce	45
Toasted Pecan Ball with Butterscotch or	
Chocolate Fudge Sauce	45
Kaufmann's Graham Cracker Ice Cream Pie	50

FRUITS IN SEASON

Mint Frosted Grapefruit Half	30
Baked Cinnamon Apple with Cream	40
Frosted Fruit Cup	35
Compote of Stewed Fruits	40

DESSERTS

Peach Pie, Lattice Top	35
French Chocolate Cream Pie	40
French Almond Cake	35

MONT BLANC: An Individual Meringue Filled with
   Whipped Cream and Puree of Marrons 35

Pave': An Extraordinarily Rich and Elegant Dessert
   Combining French Creme, Lady Fingers,
   and a Dash of Rum 35

Vacherin: This Fabulous and Traditional French Holiday
   Dessert is Made of a Delicate Pastry Filled
   with Pistachio Cream Parfait 35

BEVERAGES

Coffee, Tea or Milk	15
Iced Tea	15

Thursday Evening, December 20, 1956

Merry Christmas to All

This themed menu from December 20, 1956, celebrates Christmas in France. The store's restaurants were celebrating Christmas in a different country every day that week.

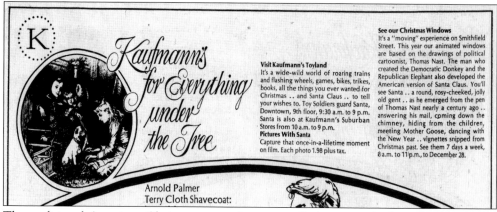

The traditional American Christmas as we know it really began in the late 1880s and early 1890s. Kaufmann's began marketing an "old-fashioned Christmas" as early as the 1930s. The store's 1975 windows were based on the drawings of Thomas Nast, the 19th century cartoonist responsible for the popular image of Santa Claus as a jolly fat man. (Courtesy of *Pittsburgh Post-Gazette* archives.)

The flagship store did not have a monopoly on Christmas cheer: the Monroeville store was also decorated for the holidays. Some of the company's suburban stores even featured window displays like those downtown.

Above, the patio shop at the Monroeville Kaufmann's was converted into the Trim-a-Home shop for the holidays. Below, the *Storagram* newsletter noted that "Santa Claus somehow manages to be at Monroeville plus Downtown at the same time greeting visitors."

This playful ad from December 20, 1964, promises a plentiful gift selection even with only four shopping days until Christmas. (Courtesy of *Pittsburgh Post-Gazette* archives.)

This 1971 image shows excited children standing in front of a Christmas window decorated with characters from the PBS show *Sesame Street*.

For many years, Kaufmann's sponsored Pittsburgh's annual Celebrate the Season parade. The pictures above show the 1983 parade along the Fifth Avenue side of the store. Below, the 1985 parade makes its way past the store with floats, balloons, and marching bands.

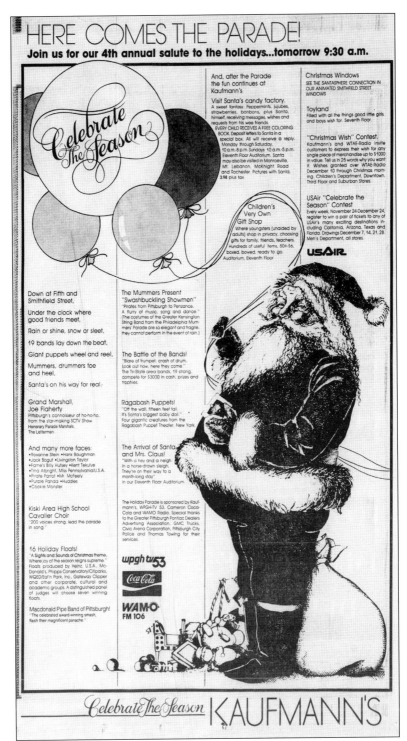

Eventually, Kaufmann's Thanksgiving Day Parade gave way to the days following that holiday. This ad for the 1984 Celebrate the Season parade shows the full slate of participants and special activities inside the store. (Courtesy of *Pittsburgh Post-Gazette* archives.)

These c. 1989 windows depict the Twelve Days of Christmas acted out by plush animals, including "six geese a-laying" (above) and "twelve lords a-leaping" (below).

12 Lords a leaping, 11 Ladies dancing, 10 Pipers piping, 9 Drummers drumming, 8 Maids a milking, 7 Swans a swimming, 6 Geese a laying, 5 Golden rings, 4 Colly birds, 3 French hens, 2 Turtle doves and a Partridge in a Pear tree

The Children's Own Shop was a seasonal department set aside specifically for children to shop for their parents and loved ones for the Christmas holidays. Displays sat at a lower eye level and featured reasonably priced trinkets and practical items, such as socks and scarves.

KAUFMANN'S
"CELEBRATE THE SEASON"
HOLIDAY EVENTS

WEDNESDAY, DEC. 2 THRU THURSDAY, DEC. 24

CHILDREN'S VERY OWN GIFT SHOP

Children between the ages of five and twelve can enjoy their own special holiday shop where they can shop for friends and family. Kaufmann's "elves" assist the children with their purchases and wrap their gifts. Items such as mugs, jewelry, toys and games (up to $10) are gift wrapped at no additional charge.

The shop is located on the seventh floor of the downtown store (adjacent to Santaland).

Hours will be:

Wed, Dec. 2 - Fri, Dec. 11........10:00am - 7:00pm
Mon, Dec. 14 - Wed, Dec. 23..10:00am - 8:00pm
All Saturdays.............................10:00am - 7:00pm
All Sundays ....10:00am - 5:30pm
Christmas Eve............................10:00am - 4:30pm

SANTALAND

Children can visit with Santa and his Elves; have a keepsake photo taken with Santa and receive a special holiday souvenir. Also, they can drop a letter to Santa in our special mailbox with direct delivery to the North Pole.

BREAKFAST, LUNCH OR DINNER WITH SANTA

Kaufmann's and OshKosh B'Gosh present "Pittsburgh's Traditional Holiday Season" performed by Winnie Flynn & Co., in the Downtown 11th Floor Auditorium. Tickets are $6.00 per person for breakfast and lunch; $7.00 per person for dinner. Reservations are required.

Call (412) 232-2175 for reservations and show dates.

This 1998 ad for special children's Christmas activities at Kaufmann's mentions the Children's Own Shop, visits with Santa, and a seasonal show in the store's 11th floor auditorium. (Courtesy of *Pittsburgh Post-Gazette* archives.)

113

This 1987 window featured children playing musical instruments around the Christmas tree.

The flagship store's first floor in the 1990s was decorated with show-stopping gold ornaments nestled in pine garlands.

The theme for 2001's windows was "The Greatest Show in Town," featuring circus scenes with many mechanical elements. These windows are immortalized in filmmaker Rick Sebak's documentary for local PBS station WQED titled *Happy Holidays in Pittsburgh*.

The 2007 Macy's windows took Cinderella as their theme, using figurines that were first displayed at Marshall Field's in Chicago.

In 2002, the Pittsburgh Ballet Theatre created a new production of *The Nutcracker*. The $2.5 million production directed by Terrence Orr featured distinctly Pittsburgh elements, one of which was a life-sized book titled *Kaufmann's Christmas Stories for Boys and Girls*. In the production, the book serves as a doorway through which fantasy creatures enter the stage. The late-19th-century book was yet another of the store's marketing tactics targeting customers of all ages. Here, the Nutcracker battles the Mouse King in a scene featuring dancer William Moore and students of the Pittsburgh Ballet Theatre School. (Courtesy of Pittsburgh Ballet Theatre.)

As the new *Nutcracker* production's main sponsor, Kaufmann's displayed a series of windows showing *The Nutcracker* story in 2002, unveiled by Pittsburgh Ballet Theatre dancers on Light-Up Night. Here is the window version of the Nutcracker–Mouse King battle.

More scenes from *The Nutcracker* windows include the international dances of France, China, Spain and Russia (above) and the dance of the snowflake fairies (below).

Though Kaufmann's officially switched to the Macy's name and corporate administration in 2006, the company carried on with its perennially popular Christmas window displays. The theme in 2008 was "A million reasons to believe." (Author's collection.)

When Macy's closed in 2015, community groups attempted to keep the tradition of the holiday windows alive. In 2016, the windows featured panels of the store's history and were decorated with boxes, bags, and wrappings from the former Kaufmann's store. (Author's collection.)

Nine

EXPANSION

Monroeville was the site of Kaufmann's first suburban store. Opened in 1960, it featured many of the places familiar to flagship store shoppers, including a Tic Toc Restaurant and Adoria Salon.

The interior of the main floor at Kaufmann's Monroeville is seen in 1960. This location was moved into Monroeville Mall in 1986 after Kaufmann's acquired several former Gimbels locations. It closed in 2006 after the Macy's takeover.

Kaufmann's second suburban location was in Mt. Lebanon, south of Pittsburgh. The store featured many upscale finishes such as wrought iron chandeliers. This store moved into South Hills Village Mall in 1986 following the company's purchase of the mall's former Gimbels location.

Ross Park Mall was among the first of Kaufmann's indoor mall locations. It was the store's second site in the North Hills. Its first store was at McKnight and Peebles Roads and opened in 1966—at that time, its third suburban location. As Kaufmann's slowly moved away from stand-alone stores, it sold the building and took over a three-story location in the mall.

Kaufmann's expanded to Northwestern Pennsylvania in 1975 with its Erie store located in Millcreek Mall.

Sibley's was a department store chain with locations in Syracuse, Rochester, and Buffalo, New York. The company merged with May Co. in 1990, and all locations took the Kaufmann's name. Kaufmann's also took over the Strouss brand in Youngstown, Ohio, as well as Hess's in Eastern Pennsylvania and Upstate New York areas.

Kaufmann's Irondequoit Mall location in Rochester, New York, came about after May Co.'s acquisition of Sibley's. This image shows the store's grand opening in the early 1990s.

Ten

LAST DAYS

In 2005, Federated Department Stores Inc. purchased May Co. and assumed control of all of its stores. In July of that year, the company announced that all former Kaufmann's stores, along with other properties Federated had acquired, would undergo a rebranding as Macy's stores. Shortly before this development, Macy's had taken over all former Lazarus locations, causing many Kaufmann's mall locations to close so as not to house two Macy's stores. (Author's collection.)

The downward spiral of the former Kaufmann's flagship continued when, in 2010, Macy's put the building up for sale with plans to rent back a certain number of floors. In 2015, it was announced that the downtown Macy's would close for good and the property would be redeveloped. Efforts were made to salvage historic artifacts and architectural elements from the store, as well as secure the rights to trademarked names like the Tic Toc Restaurant for future use. As seen below, all of the store's remaining fixtures were offered for sale. (Both, author's collection.)

KAUFMANN'S ★ macy's

KAUFMANN'S TOGETHER WITH MACY'S We're bringing you a great new place to shop. The finishing touches are almost complete. We can't wait to welcome you to your new Macy's!

This July 27, 2006, advertisement contains both the Kaufmann's and Macy's logos. The store changed names a few days later. (Courtesy of *Pittsburgh Post-Gazette* archives.)

At this writing, the former Kaufmann's building is under redevelopment as a mixed-use complex with condominiums and a hotel on the upper floors and retail spaces on the lower ones. The owners have confirmed that the new development will be known as Kaufmann's Grand on Fifth Avenue, and the bronze Kaufmann's plaques and clock will remain on the building. (Author's collection.)

BIBLIOGRAPHY

Burstin, Barbara. *Jewish Pittsburgh*. Charleston, SC: Arcadia Publishing, 2015.

Cleary, Richard. *Merchant Prince and Master Builder*. Seattle, WA: University of Washington Press, 1999.

www.fallingwater.org. Western Pennsylvania Conservancy.

Martinson, Suzanne. *The Fallingwater Cookbook: Elsie Henderson's Recipes and Memories*. Pittsburgh, PA: University of Pittsburgh Press, 2008.

Pittsburgh Post-Gazette Archives.

Pittsburgh Sun-Telegraph: Kaufmann's Supplement. May 11, 1930.

Rauh Jewish Archives, Detre Library & Archives, Senator John Heinz History Center.

ABOUT THE ORGANIZATION

The Senator John Heinz History Center is an educational institution that engages and inspires a large and diverse audience with links to the past, understanding in the present, and guidance for the future by preserving regional history and presenting the American experience with a Western Pennsylvania connection. This work is accomplished in partnership with others through archaeology, archives, artifact collections, conservation, educational programs, exhibitions, library, museums, performance, publications, research, technical assistance, and increasingly, through broadcast media and the internet. Founded in 1879 as the Historical Society of Pennsylvania, the History Center is Pittsburgh's oldest cultural organization and its exemplary Smithsonian affiliate. The collections of the Western Pennsylvania Sports Museum, the Meadowcroft Rockshelter, the Fort Pitt Museum, the Heinz History Center's Museum Collections, and the Thomas and Katherine Detre Library & Archives acquire, preserve, and make archives and artifacts available according to best practices and standards set forth by the Accreditation Commission of the American Alliance of Museums, American Library Association, and the Society of American Archivists.

The collections in the Detre Library & Archives make up an extensive repository of information on Western Pennsylvania's significant contributions to history and play a vital role in the fulfillment of the History Center's prime mission of preserving regional history and presenting the American experience with a Western Pennsylvania connection. Collecting priorities focus on materials needed for exhibits and programs, research, genealogy, and strategic initiatives. The strength is in collections representing some of the nation's most influential technological breakthroughs of the 20th century, including materials from the Westinghouse Corporation, ALCOA, H.J. Heinz Company, Carnegie Steel Company, and Jones and Laughlin Steel Corporation. Holdings continue to improve by proactively collecting relevant regional materials—maps, books, manuscripts, still and moving images, sound recordings, and oral histories—in the arts, business and commerce, ethnicity, immigration and migration, labor and industry, religion, sports, and urban development. Access to the collections is available on site during public hours, and through fee-based research services, both in-person and virtual (email, chat, and Skype). Full-text finding aids are available online from the public access catalog (www.heinzhistorycenter.org/libraryArchives) and on the Historic Pittsburgh website (digital.library.pitt.edu/pittsburgh). The Kaufmann's Department Store records are housed in dozens of archival boxes and are arranged in three series: Kaufmann's Department Store (Downtown, Pittsburgh); miscellaneous; and other department stores. The records contain advertising pieces, anniversary material, catalogs, correspondence, historical information, ledgers, newspaper clippings, pamphlets, postcards, receipts, photographs, and other sundry items. The material provides insight into the business and non-business aspects of Kaufmann's Department Store and into the Kaufmann family as well.

DISCOVER THOUSANDS OF LOCAL HISTORY BOOKS
FEATURING MILLIONS OF VINTAGE IMAGES

Arcadia Publishing, the leading local history publisher in the United States, is committed to making history accessible and meaningful through publishing books that celebrate and preserve the heritage of America's people and places.

Find more books like this at
www.arcadiapublishing.com

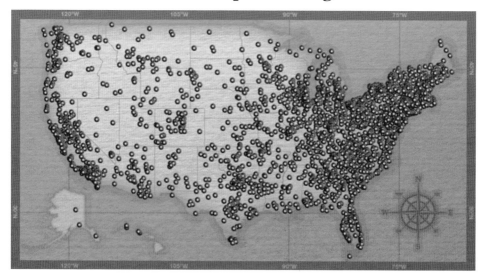

Search for your hometown history, your old stomping grounds, and even your favorite sports team.